Spelling Practice 4

by John Hedley

Schofield & Sims Ltd Huddersfield

0 7217 0382 8

First printed 1981
Reprinted 1982
Reprinted 1984
Reprinted 1985
Reprinted 1987

Designed by Peter Sinclair (Design and Print) Ltd, Wetherby
Printed in England by David Green Printers Ltd, Kettering, Northants

Words with double letters

A Read and spell.

Words with **ff**		Words with **rr**		Words with **zz**
affection	paraffin	arrest	surround	blizzard
baffling	scaffold	currency	terrace	dazzle
buffalo	suffer	irritate	tomorrow	muzzle
daffodil	suffocate	quarrel	torrent	nozzle
efficient	toffee	squirrel	warrior	puzzle

B Name each picture, using a word from the list.

C **What would happen?**
Write a word from the list to complete each sentence.
If you have a toothache, you will __1__ some pain.
If you play your records as loud as that you will __2__ the neighbours.
If you shine your torch into my eyes you will __3__ me.
If you breathe in the thick black smoke you will __4__.
If the Indians __5__ our camp we cannot escape.

D **Group words.** Write a word from the list to complete each group.
oil, petrol, __1__
yesterday, today, __2__
kindliness, love, __3__
capable, effective, __4__
perplexing, puzzling, __5__

Words ending in **ure**

A Read and spell.

failure	treasure	creature	horticulture	overture
figure	pressure	feature	lecture	picture
insure	adventure	fracture	literature	puncture
measure	agriculture	furniture	nature	temperature
pleasure	capture	future	pasture	torture

B Name each picture, using a word from the list.

1

2

3

4

5
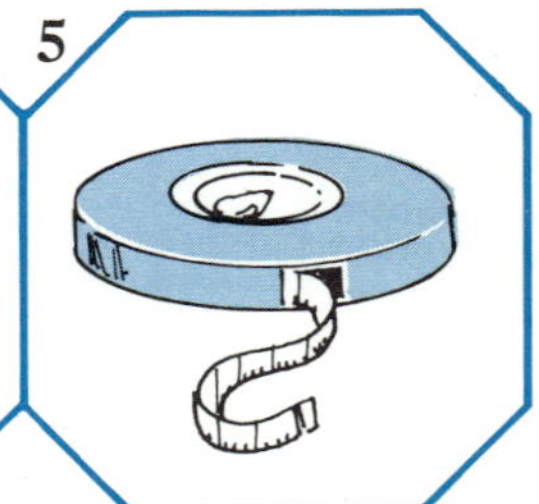

6

7

8

9

10

C **Opposites.** Write the word from the list opposite in meaning to
1 success **2** sorrow **3** past.

D **Beginnings.** 1 If the Latin word **hortus** means garden, write the word in the list meaning "cultivation of a garden".
2 If the Latin word **agri** means field, write the word in the list meaning "cultivation of a field".

E **Meanings.** Write a word from the list for each of these meanings.

___1___ – a prominent part
___2___ – grassland for feeding animals
___3___ – printed matter
___4___ – an opening piece of music
___5___ – an exciting event
___6___ – to secure payment for loss or damage

F **What are they doing?** Write a word from the list to complete each sentence.

He is checking the ___1___ of his front tyre.

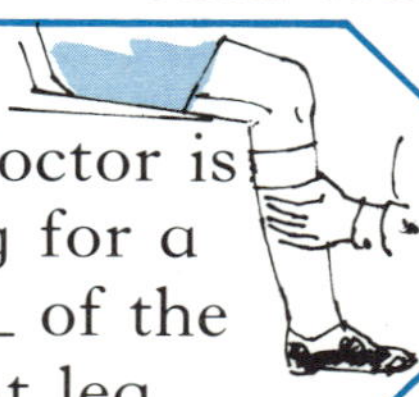
The doctor is testing for a ___2___ of the right leg.

The professor is giving a ___3___ to his students.

They are following a ___4___ trail through the forest.

Words ending in **ant** and **ent**

A Read and spell.

abundant	instant	absent	different	parent
assistant	merchant	ancient	excellent	present
attendant	pleasant	ascent	frequent	silent
fragrant	tenant	client	incident	student
important	vacant	descent	insolent	violent

B **Adjective.** Write a word from the list to complete each sentence. It must have the same meaning as the underlined word or phrase.

	A sweet-smelling rose is known as a ___1___ type.		Coffee which can be made immediately is called ___2___ coffee.
	Wayne is not here today. He is ___3___ with a cold.		The shopkeeper has a kindly manner and is always ___4___.
	The player was offensive and made ___5___ remarks.		The old castle is known as an ___6___ monument.
	The car had so many breakdowns that there were ___7___ stops.		Karen is never away. She has been ___8___ all this term.
	Plums are very plentiful and the shops have an ___9___ supply.		A high-ranking officer occupies an ___10___ position.
	When he is in a furious temper Larry can be very ___11___.		This story is so very good, I have marked it "___12___".
	No sound has been heard from the bell. It has been ___13___ for a year.	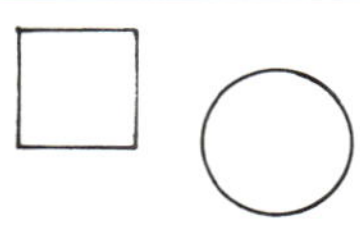	A circle is unlike a square. It is a ___14___ shape altogether.

C **Nouns.** Write a word from the list to match each of these clues.

___1___ – serves in a shop
___2___ – empty; unoccupied
___3___ – a trader
___4___ – serves in a cloakroom
___5___ – going up
___6___ – mother or father
___7___ – one who studies at college
___8___ – going down
___9___ – an event or happening
___10___ – a customer
___11___ – pays rent to a landlord

Words ending in **ance** and **ence**

A Read and spell.

advance	balance	nuisance	defence	offence
allowance	clearance	substance	evidence	pretence
ambulance	entrance	audience	existence	reference
appearance	finance	commence	licence	science
appliance	ignorance	conference	obedience	sentence

B Name each picture, using a word from the list.

C **Opposites.** Write a word from the list opposite in meaning to
1 attack **2** retreat **3** finish **4** wisdom.

D Write a word from the list to complete each sentence.

It was the comedian's first __**1**__ at the theatre.
He wondered if the __**2**__ would laugh at his jokes.

Slum __**3**__ has begun in City Road.
The council members had a __**4**__ on the site.

Teach your puppy __**5**__ from the start.
Remember, constant barking can be a __**6**__ to your neighbours.

Dad jokingly calls our spending money "high __**7**__".
We each get an __**8**__ according to our age.

The man was charged with a serious __**9**__.
The judge said he had listened to all the __**10**__.
He will pass __**11**__ tomorrow.

We have been set a test in the __**12**__ lesson. We have to say whether the white __**13**__ is flour, chalk or sugar.

The members have been discussing the possible __**14**__ of U.F.Os.

John makes a __**15**__ of knowing all the answers, and is usually wrong.
He would do better to look in a __**16**__ book first.

Words ending in **sion**

A Read and spell.

admission	decision	extension	mission	provision
collision	depression	illusion	occasion	session
conclusion	division	impression	passion	television
concussion	expansion	invasion	procession	transmission
confusion	explosion	mansion	profession	vision

B Name each picture, using a word from the list.

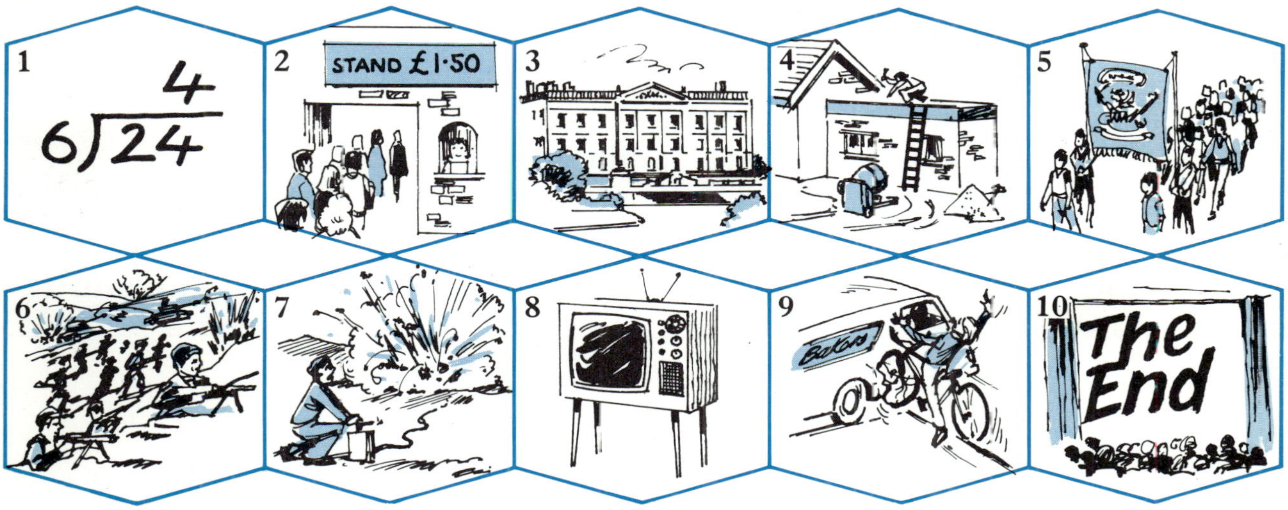

C **Nouns from verbs.** The noun **collision** is made from the verb **collide**. In the same way, find nouns in the list made from these verbs.

1 decide **2** illude **3** provide

D **Sentences.** Write a word from the list to complete each sentence.

 The room had been left in a state of __1__.	 Both boys suffered from __2__ after banging their heads together.	 After the death of his pet he had a long period of __3__.
 The spy set off on his secret __4__.	 Each of these signs stands for a __5__.	 Their silver wedding was a special __6__.
 The gap in the rails is to allow for __7__	 The pylons carry high-voltage __8__ cables.	 The netball team is arriving for a training __9__.
 This is a chart used for __10__ testing.	 Billy Bounder has a __11__ for ice cream. No wonder he is so fat!	 This is the __12__ of my little finger.

Puzzle and Progress Page

Answer each question with a word you have learned from pages 1-5.
The first letter of each answer is given.

A –double letters What am I?

My tail is bushy, I am red or grey,
I scurry up trees, My nest is a drey.
I am a s__1__.

Made of sugar and butter,
Sweet in taste and name,
For a visit to the dentist
I often take the blame.
I am a t__2__.

Soon after a winter that's bleak and cold,
I brighten the scene with my flowers of gold.
I am a d__3__.

A liquid, I give both light and heat,
I also make wax for a candle.
Used mostly in a stove, with a wick kept neat,
Which is best left for grown-ups to handle.
I am p__4__.

If your dog's a fighter,
And always in the wars,
Best to fit me
Around his jaws.
I am a m__5__.

B –ure Uses. Write a word to complete each sentence.

With a **ruler** I can m__6__ distances.

A **barometer** tells us the p__7__ of the atmosphere.

With a **repair outfit** I can mend a p__8__.

A **thermometer** tells us the t__9__.

With a **paintbox and brush** I can paint a p__10__.

C –ant or ent

Group words. Write a word similar in meaning to the rest of the group.

old, antique, aged, a__11__

chief, outstanding, noteworthy, i__12__

noiseless, quiet, soundless, s__13__

noisy, disturbing, furious, v__14__

plentiful, rich, more than enough, a__15__

D –ance or ence Notices. Write a word to complete each notice.

Dial 999
Fire
Police
a__16__

e__17__only
No Exit

AUCTION OF ANTIQUES
Sale will
c__18__
at 11 a.m.

POST OFFICE ANNOUNCEMENT
You can renew your vehicle l__19__ at any post office.

COUNTY LIBRARY
Notice to Borrowers.
Books must not be removed from the r__20__ section.

E –sion News items. Write a word to complete each sentence.

These items were on the nine o'clock news on t__21__ last night.
An e__22__ occurred due, it is thought, to a leaking gas main.
In thick fog a c__23__ took place in the Channel between two ships.
There are reports of an i__24__ of the island of Algargia by foreign troops.
After the mass meeting, members marched in p__25__ to the town hall.

Words ending in **tion**

A Read and spell.

action	destruction	fraction	nation	ration
addition	direction	imitation	operation	situation
caution	education	invention	position	solution
conversation	examination	junction	question	station
correction	fiction	motion	relation	subtraction

B Name each picture, using a word from the list.

1 49+27=

2 60−18=

3 One Fifth ⅕

4 KEEP LEFT

5 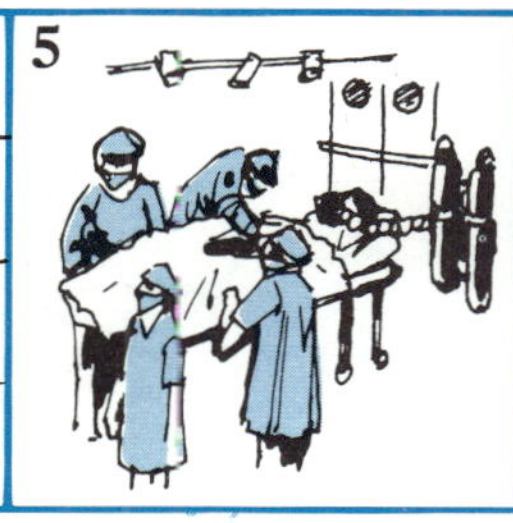

6 

7 

8 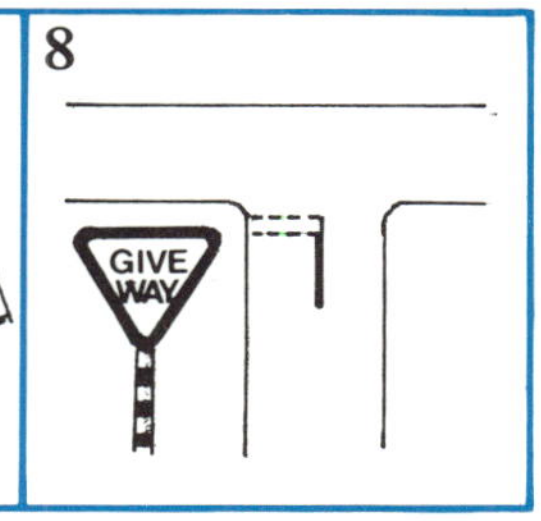

C **Group words.** Write a word from the list to complete each sentence.

To **talk**, **chat** or **gossip** is to have a ___1___ with someone.
Kicking, **punching** and **hitting** are all a kind of violent ___2___.
An ___3___ may be a **test**, an **inspection** or a **check**.
Rolling, **rocking** and **pitching** describe the ___4___ of a ship.
An **allowance**, a **share** or a **portion** mean the same as a ___5___.
Everyone of these is a ___6___ , – **mother**, **daughter** and **cousin**.

D **In other words.** Write a word from the list to complete the second comment and make it have the same meaning as the first comment.

"Get rid of it!"	"Arrange for its ___1___."
"Put it right on the programme."	"Show it as a ___2___."
"Let us see your new idea."	"Demonstrate your ___3___."
"Bring on the mimic."	"Let us see your ___4___."
"School is for your instruction,"	"and for your ___5___."
"Put the flag in the proper place."	"Fix the marker in ___6___."
"Work out the answer to this problem."	"Find the ___7___."
"Adventure stories must be in the correct section."	"They go under the heading of ___8___."
"Tell him to be more careful."	"I am giving you a ___9___."
"I want to speak to all the people."	"The President will address the ___10___."
"Offer him the job."	"The ___11___ is yours."

Words with **our**

A Read and spell.

armour	favour	labour	vapour	journey
clamour	flavour	odour	vigour	courage
colour	harbour	parlour	behaviour	flourish
detour	honour	rumour	endeavour	mourning
devour	humour	valour	splendour	tournament

B Name each picture, using a word from the list.

1
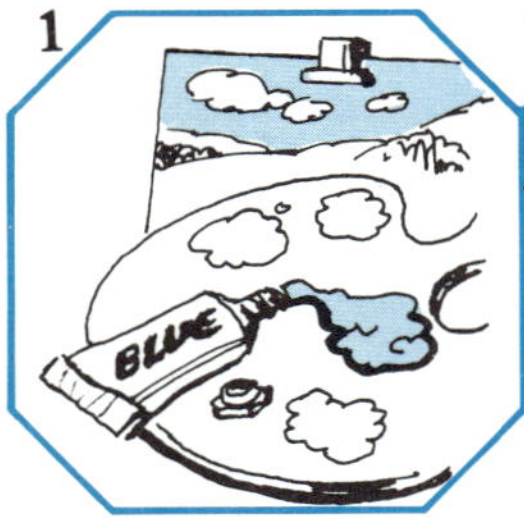

2

3
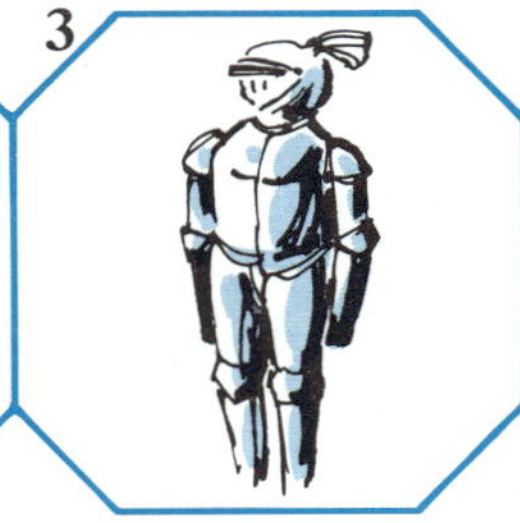

4

5

C Write **two words** from the list which mean **bravery** – __1__ and __2__.

D **One-word clues.** Write a word from the list for each of these meanings.

1 work **2** smell **3** energy **4** try **5** expedition

E **Sayings.** Write a word from the list to complete each of these sayings.
Do me a __1__ and lend me your rubber.
It is indeed an __2__ to welcome you to our school.
You need a sense of __3__ to put up with his jokes.
It is only a __4__, and I do not believe it.
Please be on your best __5__ and create a good impression.

F Write a word from the list to complete each sentence.

At feeding-time the lions __1__ for their meat, and they __2__ it very quickly.

Mother adds herbs and salt to the stew to give it that special __3__.

The cows have been trained to enter the __4__ for milking.

The firework display, in all its __5__, lit up the night sky.

The crowds are __6__ the loss of their ruler.

Feed and water the plant and it will __7__.

The world champion is taking part in the chess __8__.

Words ending in **ble** (including **ible** words)

A Read and spell.

amble	trouble	audible	incredible	responsible
bramble	grumble	divisible	impossible	reversible
noble	jumble	edible	invincible	sensible
feeble	thimble	flexible	legible	terrible
double	tremble	horrible	possible	visible

B Write a word from the list to complete each sentence.

Blackberries grow on a bush called a ___1___.

They are collecting ___2___ for a sale on Friday.

A ___3___ protects your finger when you are sewing.

When a horse moves at an easy pace, it is said to ___4___.

If you feel cold and start to ___5___, the most ___6___ thing to do is to go indoors and get warm.

C **Group words.** Complete each group with a word of the same meaning.

weak, infirm, sickly, ___1___ splendid, magnificent, impressive, ___2___

worry, disturbance, ___3___ complain, murmur, ___4___

hideous, shocking, awful, dreadful, ___5___, ___6___.

D **These can be.**

Write a word from the list to complete each explanation.

If you can hear it, it is ___1___. If you can see it, it is ___2___.

If you can eat it, it is ___3___. If you can read it, it is ___4___.

These cannot be.

If it is so surprising that you cannot believe it, it is ___5___.

If you find it so difficult that you cannot do it, it is ___6___.

If your team cannot be beaten, it is ___7___.

E Write a word from the list to complete each of these sentences.

Whoever is ___1___ for this had better own up to it.

$4 \div 4 = 1$ $8 \div 4 = 2$

$12 \div 4 = 3$ $16 \div 4 = 4$

The numbers 4, 8, 12 and 16 are all ___2___ by 4.

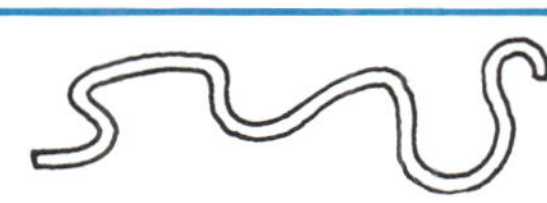

This wire is very ___3___. It will bend without breaking.

My sister has a coat which is ___4___. She can wear it inside out.

A dart in the outer ring scores ___5___.

This one scores 60, or treble 20, which is the highest ___6___ score with one dart.

Words ending in **able**

A Read and spell.

advisable	comfortable	fashionable	perishable	stable
agreeable	constable	liable	probable	suitable
cable	dependable	lovable	profitable	valuable
capable	desirable	miserable	reliable	variable
changeable	durable	noticeable	remarkable	vegetable

B Name each picture, using a word from the list.

1 
2 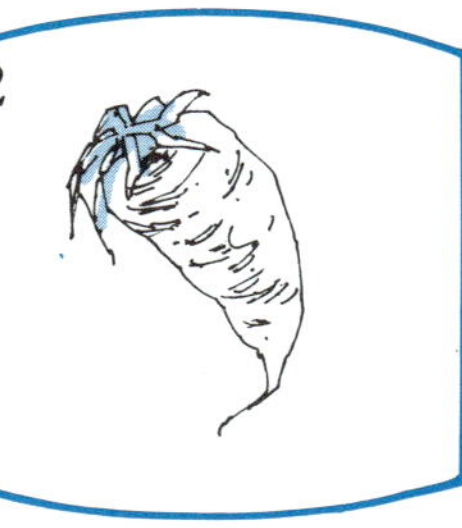
3 
4 

C Write the **opposite** of
1 unwanted
2 happy
3 unlikely
4 unnoticed.

D **Two words with the same meaning.**
Write words from the list to complete these sentences.
If weather, on the same day, is warm and dry and then becomes cool and wet, we say it is __1__ or __2__.
A friend who can be relied upon is both __3__ and __4__.
Although you may think it __5__ to sell your stamp collection now, I would keep it as the stamps are sure to become more __6__.

E **Sentences.** Write words from the list to complete these sentences.

The doctor thought it was __1__ for me to have an X-ray. My parents were __2__ and took me to the hospital.

Anne is a most __3__ player. She scored a __4__ hat trick of goals within five minutes.

Concrete is very hard and __5__, – it lasts a long time. Most fruit is soft and __6__, – it soon starts to decay.

These shoes may well be __7__ and most girls like to wear them, but they are not really __8__ for school.

We always let Grandpa have the most __9__ chair.

ROAD
__10__ TO
SUBSIDENCE

This sign means that parts of the road may sink down.

Kay found all the puppies so __11__ she did not know which one to choose.

Words with silent letters

A Read and spell.

Words with a silent **b**			Words with a silent **k**		
bomb	doubtful	plumber	knack	knit	knowledge
climb	dumb	thumb	knave	knob	knuckle
comb	lamb	tomb	knee	knock	
crumb	limb		knife	knot	
debt	numb		knight	know	

B Name each picture, using a word from the list.

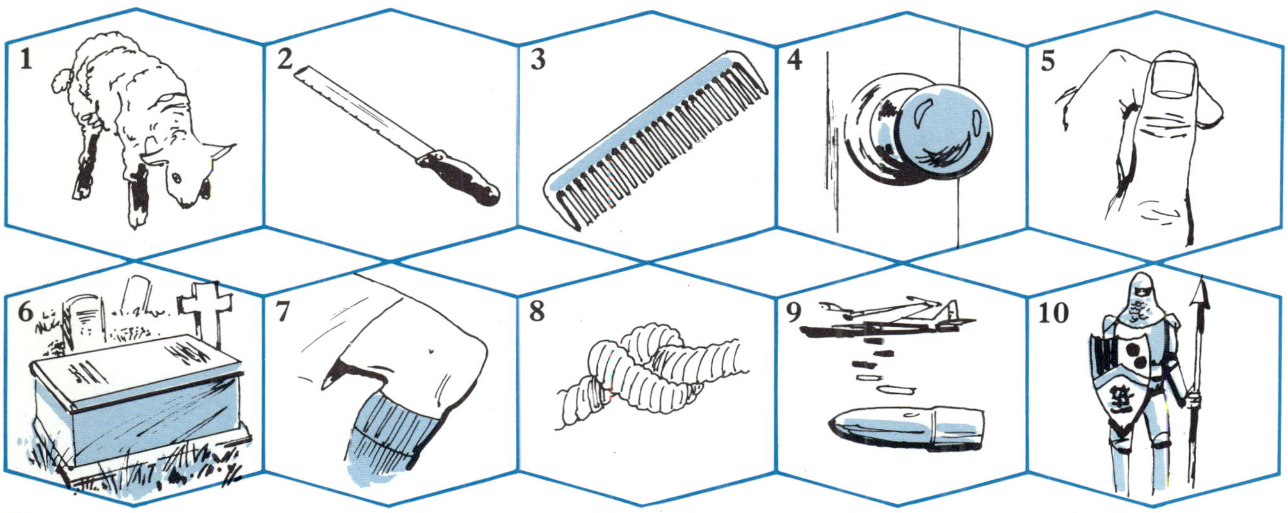

C **Meanings.** Write a word from the list for each of these meanings.

___1___ – a small fragment of bread

___2___ – an arm or a leg or a branch

___3___ – to recognize or identify

___4___ – the bone at a finger joint

D Write a word from the list to complete each of these sentences.

If you owe money, you are in ___1___.
If you are uncertain or undecided, you are ___2___.
A person unable to speak is ___3___.
If your fingers are ___4___ with cold, you have no feeling in them.
A ___5___ fits and repairs water pipes, taps and cisterns.
If a person has the trick of doing something skilfully, we say he has a ___6___ for it.
You can gain ___7___ from books, lessons, radio, and television.
A dishonest person may be called a rogue or a ___8___.

E **Actions.** Write a word from the list for which each picture is a clue.

Puzzle and Progress Page

Answer each question with a word you have learned from pages 7-11. The first letter of each answer is given.

A –tion **Places.** Write a word to complete each sentence.

A s____1____ is a stopping-place on the railway.
A hospital is a place where an o____2____ may be performed.
A j____3____ is a place where tracks or roads meet.
A school is a place where e____4____ is given.
A boxing ring is where a good deal of a____5____ takes place.

B – our **Group words.** Write a word to complete each description.

Red, yellow, and orange. Each of these is a c____6____.
Vanilla, raspberry, strawberry. Each of these is an ice cream f____7____.
Port, shelter, dock. Each is a kind of h____8____ for ships.
Trip, expedition, outing. Each is a kind of j____9____.
Work, industry, task. Each means the same as l____10____.

C –ble **In other words.** Write a word to complete the second statement.

I can see it. It is just v____11____.
I can twist and bend the hose-pipe. It is f____12____.
I must not complain or be grumpy about it. I must not g____13____.
I look, walk and talk exactly like my brother. I am his d____14____.
The baby has not cried or wanted any attention. She has been no t____15____.

D –able **Adjectives.** Write a word to complete each sentence.

Use a cushion if you want to be more c____16____.

Choose a watch that is r____18____ – one that keeps good time.

Wear s____20____ boots when you go rock climbing.

Beards are very f____17____ this year.

The bible is chained because it is old and very v____19____.

E – Silent letters. What am I?

A fork is my partner
For most of my life,
I am not a spade
I am a k____21____.

Compared with your fingers,
I usually come
Shorter and thicker,
I am your t____22____.

Tied tightly on parcels,
I am used a lot
In string or cord,
I am a k____23____.

If your hair is unruly and apt to roam,
Put it back in place with me.
I am a c____24____.

My mother is a ewe, my father is a ram,
I am the young of the family and called a l____25____.

Words with silent letters

A Read and spell.

Words with a silent g
design, gnaw, foreigner, gnome, gnarled, neigh, gnash, sign, gnat, sovereign

Words with a silent w
wrangle, wrench, wrinkles, wrap, wrestling, wrist, wreath, wretched, write, wreck, wriggle, wrong, wren, wring, wheelwright

B Name each picture, using a word from the list.

1 
2 
3 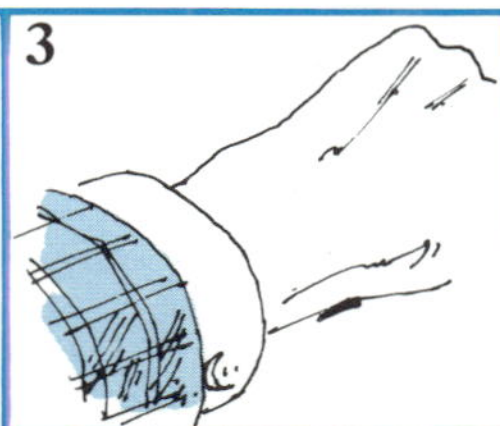
4 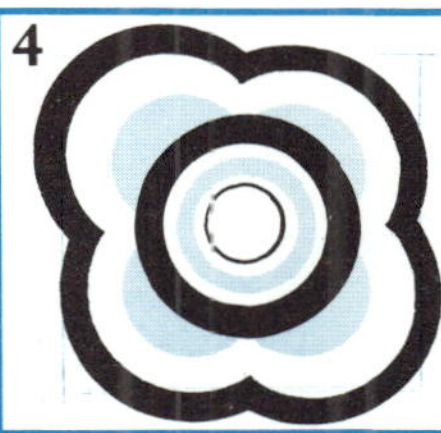
5 
6 
7 
8 
9 
10 

C **Meanings.** Write a word from the list for each of these.

___1___ – one who comes from another country
___2___ – to form letters with a pen or pencil
___3___ – miserable, unhappy
___4___ – incorrect, unlawful

D **Actions.** Write a word from the list to complete each sentence.

An ape will ___1___ its teeth when it is angry or excited.

A dog loves to ___2___ at a bone.

A horse will ___3___ when it hears another approaching.

I will ___4___ this blanket around you.

They always ___5___ over who is to bat first.

He tried to ___6___ the door open.

She had to ___7___ through the hole in the fence.

You must ___8___ out the cloth before using it again.

E **Old-timers.** Write a word to complete each description.

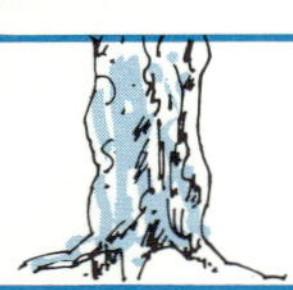
The old tree has a ___1___ trunk.

A gold ___2___ is a valuable old coin.

Very old people often have ___3___ in their skin.

Words with silent letters

A Read and spell.

Words with a silent **u**		Words with a silent **i**	Words with a silent **l**	
build	guess	bruise	almond	folk
guild	guest	fruit	chalk	halfpenny
biscuit	guide	juice	stalk	could
disguise	guilty	pursuit	talk	should
guard	tongue	suit	walk	would

B Name each picture, using a word from the list.

C **Sentences.** Write a word from the list to complete each sentence.
Today I **can** swim one length. Last week I __1__ only swim one width.

Next week I **shall** try for two lengths. I __2__ not find it too difficult.

Will you come and see me do it? It __3__ encourage me if you did.

D **Group words.** Write a word from the list in its correct group.
chat, gossip, __1__
stroll, saunter, __2__
construct, erect, __3__
people, persons, __4__
chase, hunt, __5__

E **Meanings.** Write a word from the list for each of these meanings.
__1__ – kernel of a stone-fruit
__2__ – a group or society of people
__3__ – a person invited to your house
__4__ – to estimate roughly
__5__ – discolouring of the skin caused by a blow
__6__ – the liquid part of a fruit or vegetable
__7__ – responsible for committing an offence

Words beginning with **dis**

A Read and spell.

disabled	discount	disgust	dismiss	distance
disarm	discover	disinfectant	disperse	distinct
disaster	discuss	dismal	display	distress
disclose	disease	dismantle	dispute	district
discord	disgrace	dismay	dissolve	disturb

B **Nouns.** Write a word from the list to complete each sentence.

This milestone gives the ___1___ to London.

This plant is suffering from a root ___2___.

The reduction of 25% is called a ___3___.

Playing a wrong note can produce ___4___.

A volcano erupting is a natural ___5___.

An aircraft in trouble sends out a ___6___ signal.

A ___7___ is used to clean drains.

He is filled with ___8___ at having missed a penalty.

He has a look of ___9___ on his face when he sees the work of vandals.

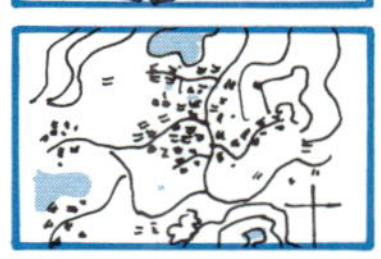

This is a map of the village and the surrounding ___10___.

C **Verbs.** Write a word from the list for each meaning.

___1___ – to take weapons away

___2___ – to reveal or make known

___3___ – to find out

___4___ – to debate or talk about

___5___ – to take to pieces

___6___ – to bring shame or dishonour

___7___ – to become liquid

___8___ – to scatter in all directions

___9___ – to exhibit or put on show

___10___ – to argue or question a decision

___11___ – to send away or discard

___12___ – to worry or break someone's rest

D **Adjectives.** Write a word from the list to complete each sentence.

It is ___1___ weather outside, with this fog and drizzle.

He is ___2___ as the result of a road accident.

Footprints in fresh snow are quite ___3___.

Words beginning with **dis**

(where **dis** is a prefix used to make the word opposite in meaning, for example **dis+obey** makes disobey)

A Read and spell.

disability	disapproval	disconnect	dishonest	disorder
disadvantage	disarranged	discontented	dislike	displaced
disagree	disbelieve	disembark	disloyal	displease
disallowed	discoloured	disfigured	dismount	dissatisfied
disappear	discomfort	disheartened	disobedient	distrust

B Write a word or words from the list to complete each sentence.

The magician will make the bird in the cage ____1____.

The pile of tins has been ____2____, and the whole store is in a state of ____3____.

Please remember to ____4____ the plug when you have finished.

The statue has been ____5____ by vandals.

Each of these is suffering from a ____6____.

When you come off a ship you ____7____.

When you get off a bicycle you ____8____.

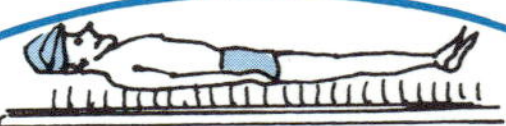

The Indian fakir feels no pain or ____9____ on his bed of nails.

The first glass of water looked dirty and ____10____.

I think your story is untrue. In fact, I ____11____ every word of it.

If you are ____12____ because it is faulty, then take it back to the shop.

It is sometimes a ____13____ to buy the cheapest model. It is more likely to go wrong.

My entry for the painting competition arrived late and was ____14.____.

A traitor is ____15____ to his country. A cheat is ____16____ in his dealings.

The teacher expresses ____17____ of my work by writing "Not good enough" on it.

I enjoy most of the group's records, but I ____18____ their latest one.

My friend is stubborn and we often ____19____ about the smallest things.

If you are happy you are contented. If you are unhappy you are ____20____.

When your team wins you feel heartened by their victory. When they lose you feel ____21____ by their defeat.

Good manners please everyone, but bad manners ____22____ most people.

Refugees are those who have been ____23____ from their own land.

You can trust a friend, but you may ____24____ a stranger.

One who refuses to carry out an order is ____25____.

Words beginning with a **prefix**

A Read and spell.

Words beginning with **im** or **in**, meaning **not**	Words beginning with **mis** meaning **wrongly** or **badly**	Words beginning with **sub** meaning **under** or **below**	Words beginning with **super** meaning **above** or **greater**	Words beginning with **tri** meaning **three**
impatient	misbehave	submarine	superfine	triangle
imperfect	misfire	subnormal	superhuman	tricycle
inattentive	misfit	subsoil	supermarket	trident
incapable	misfortune	subsonic	supersonic	trimaran
invisible	mislead	subway	superstructure	tripod

B Name each picture, using a word from the list.

C **Meanings.** Write a word from the list for each of these.

___1___ – faulty ___2___ – bad luck ___3___ – to act badly
___4___ – below the speed of sound ___5___ – above the speed of sound
___6___ – upper part of a building ___7___ – below or less than usual
___8___ – cannot be seen ___9___ – not paying attention

D Write a word from the list to complete each sentence.

Some people in the queue were growing ___1___.

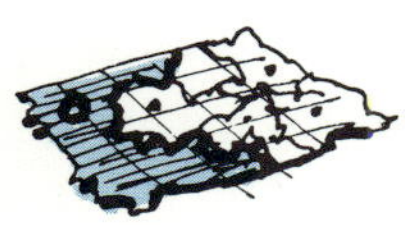

The map is old and out of date. It will ___3___ you.

This margarine is of the highest possible quality. That is why it is called ___5___.

This rifle is perfect and has never been known to ___2___.

Boris, the strong man, claims to have ___4___ strength.

Tony has sprained his ankle and he is ___6___ of walking any further.

Puzzle and Progress Page

Answer each question with a word you have learned from pages 13-17. The first letter of each answer is given.

A **Rearrange the letters** to write a word with the given meaning.

t a n g – a small insect – g___1___
s i n g – a name board on an inn – s___2___
c r e w k – a badly damaged ship – w___3___
s t i r w – joins hand to arm – w___4___
g r o w n – the opposite of right – w___5___

B **Where they may be found.**
From the clues, write the name of each object.

A g___6___ may be on a train or in front of an open fire.
A g___7___ may be directing mountaineers or tourists.
F___8___ may be on the branch of an apple, a pear or a plum tree.
A t___9___ may be inside a mouth or in the opening of a boot or shoe.
T___10___ is heard in a conversation, a speech or a discussion.

C **Newspaper placards.**
Write the word beginning with **dis** to which each of these refer.

d___11___ d___12___ d___13___ d___14___ d___15___

D **Meanings of verbs.** Write the correct verb for each meaning.

dism___16___ – to get down from a horse
disb___17___ – to think something is untrue
disa___18___ – to differ or quarrel
disl___19___ – to have no love for
disc___20___ – to untie or unfasten

E **Puzzle rhymes.** Write the word to complete each rhyme.

Be good! Be quiet! Be like young Dave!
He has never been known to m___21___.

My space gun works in a wonderful way,
You cannot see its i___22___ ray.

An underground path below the busy street
The s___24___ echoes to pedestrians' feet.

Stocked with goods on numerous shelves,
A s___25___ is where shoppers serve themselves.

A shape often seen on road signs,
Made up of three straight lines,
Or an instrument held in the hand,
A t___23___ is part of a percussion band.

Words beginning with a **prefix**

A Read and spell.

Words with **en** meaning **in, into**	Words with **fore** meaning **in front, before**		Words with **re** meaning **again**	Words with **tele** meaning **far, distant**
enclose	forearm	foreground	rebuild	telegram
encode	forecast	forehead	recommence	telegraph
endangered	forecourt	foreman	refuel	telephone
enlist	forefeet	forename	replay	telescope
entangled	forefinger	foresee	rewrite	television

B Name each picture, using a word from the list.

1
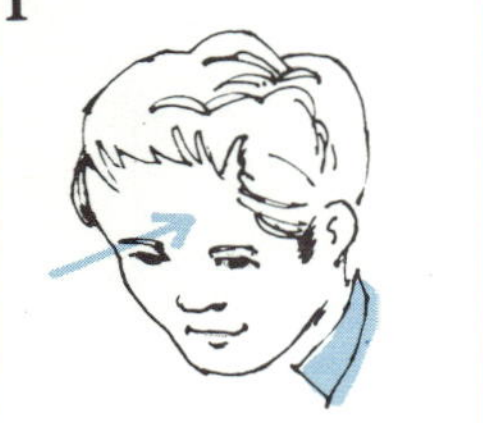
2
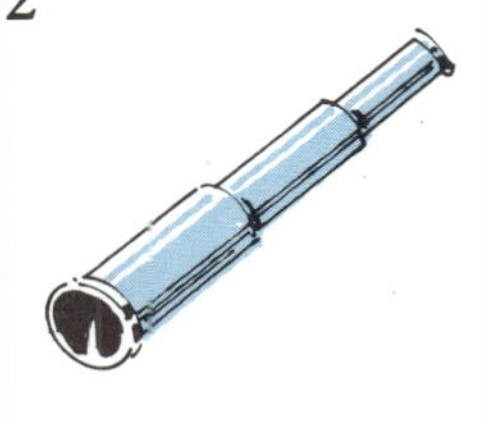
3
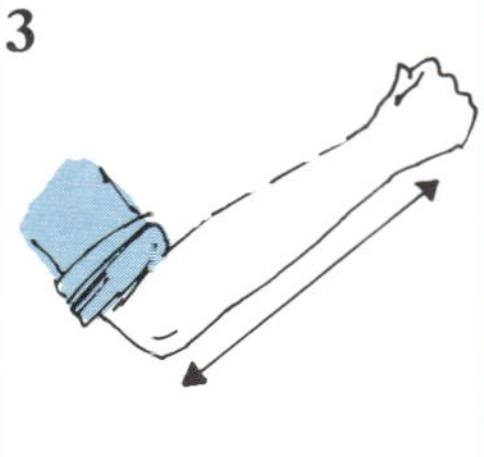
4
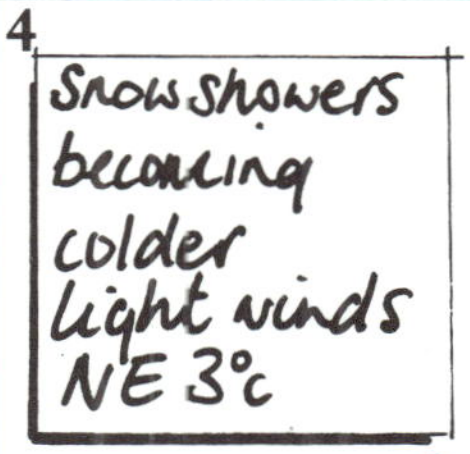

5

6

7
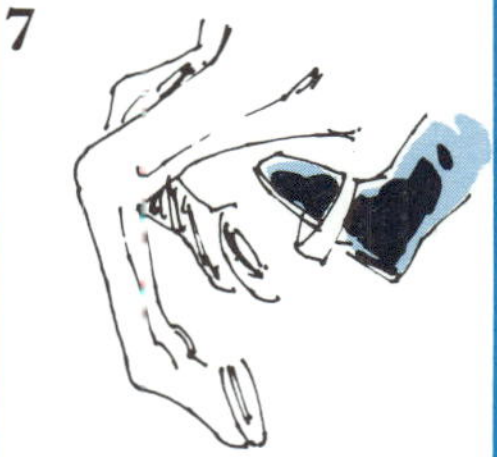
8

9

10
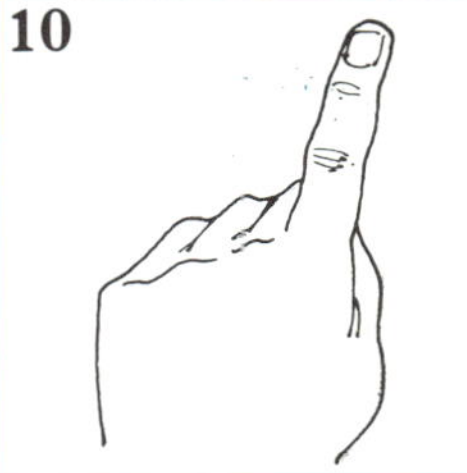

C **Meanings.** Write a word from the list for each of these.
___1___ – to put into secret writing ___2___ – to see or know beforehand
___3___ – an overseer in charge of workers ___4___ – to join the army

D Write a word from the list to complete each of these sentences.
Please ___1___ a stamped, addressed envelope.
In our class the most popular ___2___ for girls is Anne.
After a goaless draw the ___3___ will be on Wednesday next.
There were so many mistakes in my letter that I had to ___4___ it.
The ___5___ said: "Arriving 8 p.m. Stop Please meet train".
Marconi invented the wireless ___6___.
The raiders became ___7___ in the coils of barbed wire.

They began to ___8___ the damaged house until bad weather stopped them. Work will ___9___ soon.

As a result of so much slaughter, the whale has now become an ___10___ animal.

This picture shows the mansion with a lake in the ___11___.

Words beginning with **ex**
(**ex-** is a Latin **prefix** meaning **from**, **out of**)

A Read and spell.

exact	excitement	exhausted	expedition	export
excavate	exclaim	exhibit	experience	exterior
exceed	excursion	exile	experiment	extinguisher
except	excuse	exit	expert	extra
exchange	exercise	expect	explain	extract

B Name each picture, using a word from the list.

1

2

3

4

5

C **Meanings.** Write a word from the list for each of these.

___1___ – to cry out ___2___ – tired out ___3___ – the opposite of interior
___4___ – one who is absent from his own country ___5___ – pardon
___6___ – goods sent out of a country ___7___ – way out
___8___ – to make the meaning plain ___9___ – a skilful person

D Write a word from the list to complete each of these sentences.

The carnival created a lot of ___1___ in the district.
It was a new ___2___ for Jane to be one of the attendants.
All the family were there ___3___ Tommy. He had an appointment with the dentist who was due to ___4___ one of his teeth. I ___5___ we shall hear all about it.
He will get an ___6___ helping of cake – if he can eat it!

E Write a word from the list to complete each of these notices.

It is an offence to ___1___ the speed limit.

This superb watch will always tell you the ___2___ time.

___3___ your gift tokens here.

Join our weekday ___4___ to London.

Pedal power saves petrol and gives healthy ___5___.

Words beginning with a soft **c**
(where **c** is sounded as **s**)

A Read and spell.

cease	cemetery	cider	circuit	civilian
cedar	centre	cigarette	circus	cyclone
celery	century	cinders	cistern	cygnet
cell	ceremony	cinema	citizen	cylinder
cement	certain	cipher	citrus	cymbal

B Name each picture, using a word from the list.

C **Meanings.** Write a word from the list for each meaning.

__1__ – a building where films are shown __2__ – a wind storm
__3__ – to give over, stop or end __4__ – sure, not to be doubted
__5__ – embers left after burning coal

D Write a word from the list to complete each sentence.

Food and drink. __1__ is a drink made from apples.
__2__ is a plant with white stalks for eating.
Lemons, limes, oranges and grapefruit are all __3__ fruits.

People. A __4__ is a townsman or inhabitant of a city.
When he leaves the army a soldier becomes a __5__ again.
A priest can perform the wedding __6__ in a church.

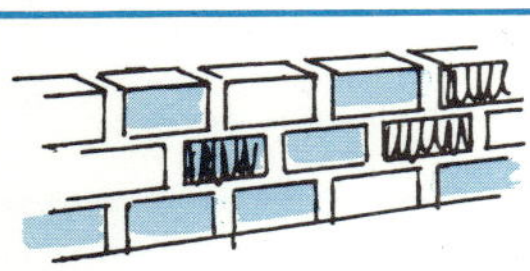	Mortar is made from sand, __7__ and water.		The ball is placed on the __8__ spot ready for kick-off.
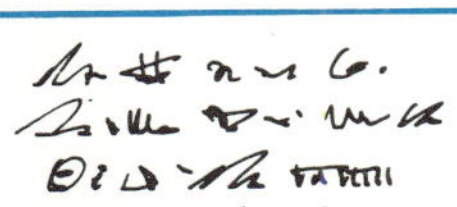	This is in __9__, or secret writing.		He had to retire after one __10__ of the track.

Words with **ge**, **gi** or **gy** sounding as **j**

A Read and spell.

generous	giant	gymnasium	imagine	pigeon
genius	gigantic	gypsy (or gipsy)	indigestion	regiment
gentle	ginger	apology	legend	region
geography	giraffe	college	longitude	surgery
geometry	gymkhana	engine	oxygen	tragedy

B Name each picture, using a word from the list.

C **Opposites.**
Write a word from the list opposite in meaning to each of these.
mean – ____1____ rough – ____2____ tiny – ____3____ comedy – ____4____

D **At school.** Write words from the list to complete these sentences.
We study the earth and its people. This is called ____1____. The maps we use have lines of latitude and ____2____. As part of mathematics, we learn about ____3____ when we study lines, angles and shapes.
For exercises and games practice we use the ____4____.
Keith is a brilliant pianist. In fact, we call him a ____5____.
He hopes, later, to go to a ____6____ of music.

E **Meanings.** Write a word from the list for each meaning.
____1____ – a hot-tasting substance ____2____ – a body of soldiers
____3____ – an area or district ____4____ – a traditional story
____5____ – to think or form an image in your mind
____6____ – an expression of your regret, such as "I am sorry"

F **Speech.** Write words from the list to complete each sentence.

"Let me fit your ____1____ cylinder ready for the final climb."

"I have entered him for three events at the local ____2____."

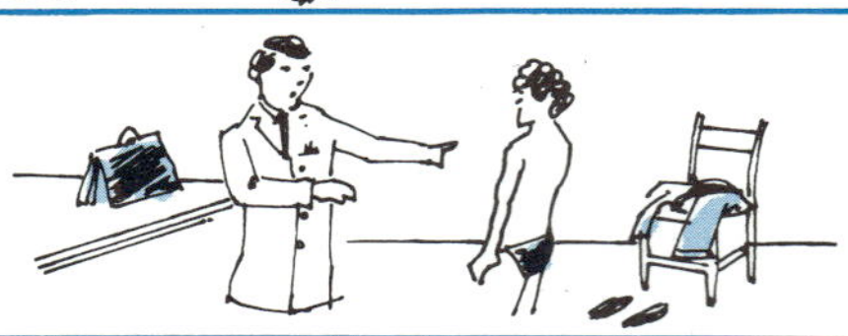

"Your stomach ache is due to a bout of ____3____. I will see you again at my ____4____ on Friday night."

Words with **au**

A Read and spell.

applause	Australia	autumn	launch	somersault
astronaut	Austria	cauliflower	laundrette	tarpaulin
auburn	authority	exhaust	precaution	aunt
auction	autograph	fraud	saucer	beautiful
August	automatic	haulage	sausage	gauge

B Name each picture, using a word from the list.

C **Partners.** Write a word from the list to complete each of these.

cup and ___1___ ___2___ and uncle

D **One word clues.** Write a word from the list to fit each of these.

___1___ – colour ___2___ – country ___3___ – season

___4___ – signature ___5___ – month

E Write a word from the list to complete each sentence.

An ___1___ machine works on its own.

A ___2___ is a cheat who carries out a trick by deception.

A ___3___ object is one that is very pleasing to look at.

A ___4___ is used for measuring.

A person in ___5___ is one who is in charge and gives orders.

Before the aircraft takes off, you should take the ___6___ of fastening your seat-belt.

Mr. Robson has a fleet of lorries and is a well-known ___7___ contractor.

The acrobat is performing a ___8___.

Puzzle and Progress Page

Answer each question with a word you have learned from pages 19-23. The first letter or letters of each answer is given.

A **Requests.** Write a word to complete each of these.

Please e__1__ two photographs with your passport application.
He f__2__ the results correctly and quickly despatched a t__3__.
Do you view children's t__4__ regularly?
As your written story is far too untidy will you please r__5__ it.

B **Advice.** Write a word to complete each sentence.

The old coin may be valuable. Ask an ex__6__ to value it.
The fire brigade will tell you which type of ex__7__ is best to use.
It is unwise to ex__8__ with chemicals without proper supervision.
To make the lid a perfect fit, cut it to the ex__9__ measurements.
Your dog is too fat. Give it less food and more ex__10__.

C **Three clues for one word.**

c__11__ – one hundred Roman soldiers, 100 years, 100 runs
c__12__ – wedding, prize-giving, laying a foundation-stone
c__13__ – clowns, acrobats, performing animals
c__14__ – crosses, headstones, memorials
c__15__ – in a prison, in a monastery, in a honeycomb

D **What am I?**

Mighty and fearsome, on my strength I'm reliant.
I may look human, but I am really a g__16__.

At my very long neck
Perhaps you will laugh, –
But I see more of the world,
And enjoy being a g__17__.

With my dark hair and skin,
And my caravan as well,
I am a g__18__ who, for silver,
Your fortune will tell.

The doctor won't be long,
He is just a trifle late.
He will see you in his s__19__
If you will kindly wait.

A clever bird am I,
A p__20__ is my name,
For finding my way home
Is my chief claim to fame.

E **Places.** Write a word to complete each sentence.

The a__21__ is walking in space.

The kangaroo is a native of A__22__.

The vase is being sold by a__23__ in the sale-room.

She is giving her a__24__ to one of her fans at the stage door.

The l__25__ takes trippers up the river.

Words with **ua**

A Read and spell.

actually	estuary	January	quality	squabble
annually	February	language	quantity	squad
aquarium	gradual	manual	quarry	squall
continual	guarantee	persuade	quarter	truant
earthquake	individual	punctual	situated	usually

B Name each picture, using a word from the list.

C **Time Words.** Write the words from the list to complete these sentences.
The first two months of the year, in correct order, are ___1___ and ___2___.
An event occurring every year takes place ___3___.
To be ___4___ is to arrive at the exact time, but a bad timekeeper is ___5___ late.
___6___ rain goes on without stopping.
A ___7___ improvement in the weather means it is getting better by stages or 'grades'.

D **Meanings.** Write a word from the list for each of these.
___1___ – human speech ___2___ – truly, really
___3___ – used by the hand (from the Latin **manus**)
___4___ – to cause someone to believe, to convince
___5___ – a single one, a separate one, a particular one
___6___ – one who is absent from school without excuse

E **The world about us.** Identify each of these using a word from the list.
___1___ – a shaking of the earth ___2___ – a short violent wind
___3___ – the tidal mouth of a large river

F **Advertisements.** Write a word from the list to complete each of these.

Just arrived
A large selection of scarves made from the finest ___1___ silk.

Each **radio** carries a two-year ___2___.

Stock up for winter!
Any ___3___ of coalite delivered to your door. Ring 73658

Flat for sale
Conveniently ___4___ near town centre.

Words with **ph** which is pronounced as **f**

A Read and spell.

phantom	phrase	elephant	orphan	siphon
pharmacy	physical	epitaph	pamphlet	sphere
pheasant	alphabet	graph	paragraph	sphinx
Philip	atmosphere	microphone	prophet	triumph
photograph	cenotaph	nephew	semaphore	typhoon

B Name each picture, using a word from the list.

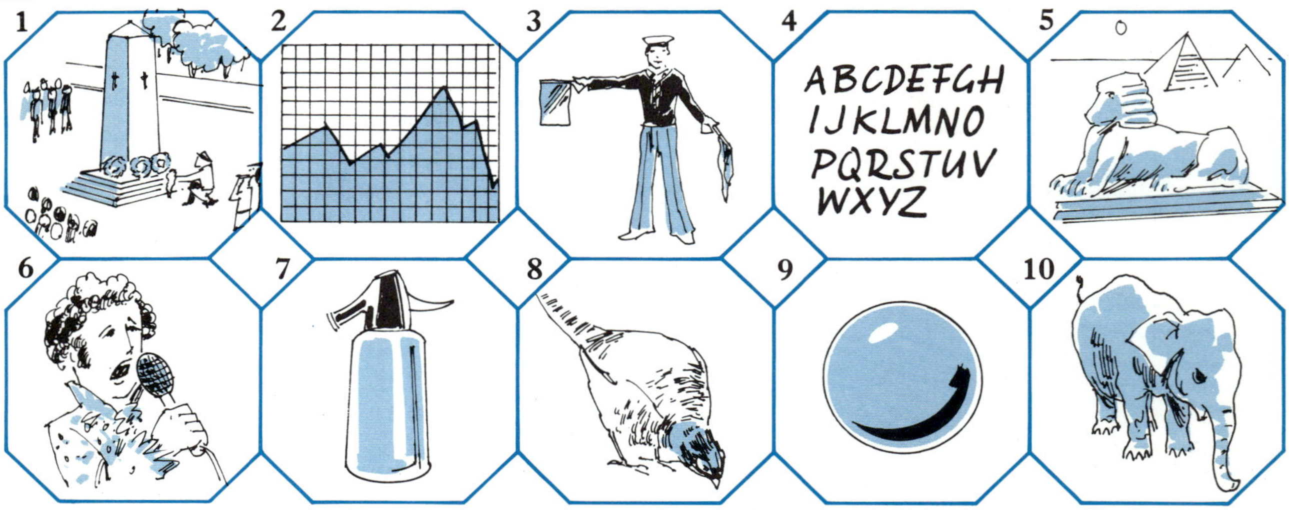

C **People.** Write a word from the list for each of these.

__1__ – a boy's name __2__ – the son of a brother or sister

__3__ – one who has lost both parents

__4__ – one who foretells the future

D **Meanings.** Write a word from the list for each meaning.

__1__ – complete victory __2__ – ghost __3__ – booklet, leaflet

__4__ – group of sentences, separate item in a newspaper

__5__ – a small group of words __6__ – violent storm, whirlwind

__7__ – an envelope of gas surrounding the Earth

E **Word and picture clues.** Write a word from the list to match each one.

Prescriptions

__1__

Taken on film

__2__

Memorial words

__3__

P.E. lesson

__4__ education

Words with y

A Read and spell.

buying	bury	mystery	pyjamas	symphony
copying	bypass	nylon	pyramid	syringe
dyeing	canyon	oyster	rhythm	syrup
flying	enemy	poetry	sycamore	typist
trying	hymn	pygmy (or pigmy)	sympathy	tyrant

B Name each picture, using a word from the list.

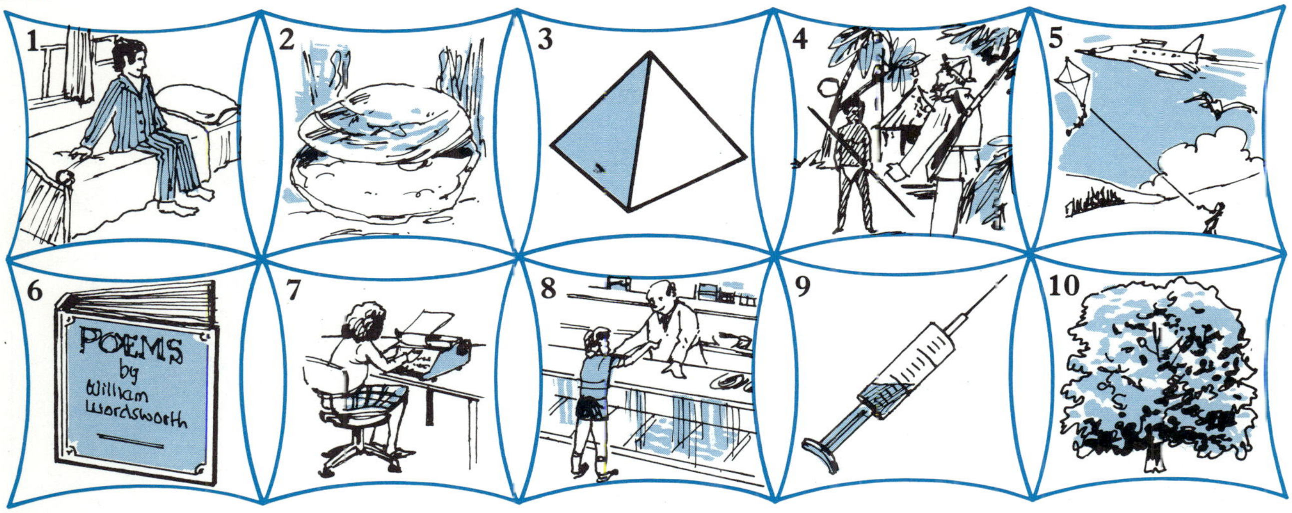

C **Music words.** Write a word from the list to complete each sentence.
A ___1___ is a song of praise sung in religious service.
A ___2___ is a large work played by an orchestra.
Drums beat out the ___3___ of a tune, keeping a pattern of long and short sounds.

D **Meanings.** Write a word from the list for each of these.
___1___ – to hide in the ground ___2___ – foe
___3___ – thick, sweet liquid ___4___ – a bully; a cruel ruler
___5___ – pity; a close feeling for another
___6___ – a man-made fibre used for brushes, sheets and stockings
___7___ – a deep gorge or ravine
___8___ – a secret; something not understood

E **Action.** Write a word from the list to complete each sentence.

After ___1___ the sheet a different colour, she will hang it out to dry.

They are building a ___2___ to carry traffic round the busy town.

She is ___3___ on a new pair of shoes.

Look out! Kevin is ___4___ your answers.

French words now used in the English language

A Read and spell.

amateur	baton	bureau	capsule	champagne
antique	boulevard	cabaret	cassette	chauffeur
automobile	bouquet	cadet	catalogue	coupon
ballet	boutique	café	cavalcade	debris
banquet	buffet	camouflage	centimetre	depot

B Name each picture, using a word from the list.

C **Food and drink.** Write a word from the list for each meaning.

__1__ – a rich feast __2__ – white sparkling wine

__3__ – a meal set out on tables for diners to help themselves.

__4__ – entertainment given in a restaurant

__5__ – originally a coffee-house, now a tea-house or restaurant

D Write a word from the list to complete each sentence.

Opposites.

A **professional** is paid for his services but an __1__ is unpaid.

Anything **modern** is of recent times but an __2__ is of an old age.

In the town.

A __3__ is a broad main road, usually bordered with trees.

A __4__ is a small shop or department, usually selling clothes.

Buses return to the __5__ after their daily services.

E **Meanings.** Write a word beginning with **ca** from the list to complete each sentence.

If you buy goods by mail-order, you select them from a __1__.

A __2__ is a spacecraft or a case holding a dose of medicine.

A pop tune may be recorded on a disc or on tape in a __3__.

A police __4__ is a young person training for the police force.

A parade of vehicles or riders on horseback is called a __5__.

More French words now used in the English language

A Read and spell.

encore	limousine	monocle	restaurant	satellite
guillotine	machine	omelette	ricochet	silhouette
horoscope	massacre	parachute	rosette	souvenir
hotel	matinee	portrait	rouge	tonne
kilometre	menu	prairie	sabotage	troupe

B Name each picture, using a word from the list.

C Write a word from the list to complete each sentence.

Measures. A ___1___ is a length of one thousand metres.
A ___2___ is a weight of one thousand kilograms.

Wrongdoing. The tyrant ordered the ___3___ of everyone in the village.
Dynamite had been used to ___4___ the power-station.

Precautions. To be sure of a room for the night, ring the ___5___ now.
To be sure of a meal, book a table at the ___6___ now.

Actions.  The artist is painting a ___7___.

The actor gives a nightly performance and a ___8___ on Thursday at 2.30 p.m.

The cook is making an ___9___.

In North America, the covered wagons took many days to cross the ___10___.

To redden his cheeks the clown uses ___11___.

The scientists have launched another ___12___ into orbit round the Earth.

As an ___13___ the soloist sang a verse and a chorus.

For three francs Paul bought a ___14___ of his French visit.

With care you can make a flat stone ___15___ off the surface of the water.

Puzzle and Progress Page

Answer each question with a word you have learned from pages 25-29. The first letter of each answer is given.

A **What happens here?** Write a word to complete each sentence.

In an a__1__ fish swim and water plants grow within glass walls.
In an e__2__ the ground heaves due to faults in the Earth's crust.
In an e__3__ boats enter the river from the sea.
In a q__4__ stone is dug or blasted out.
In a s__5__ people have a noisy, petty quarrel.

B **What am I?**

Reared as a game-bird,
(For me the game is not fun),
Set free in the woodland,
Preen in the sun.
I am a p__6__.

"Testing. Testing. One, two, three."
I am ready for action. Speak into me.
I am a m__7__.

If bubbling soda-water
You would wish to drink,
Press my lever down quite gently,
I squirt it quicker than you think.
I am a s__8__.

You are most likely to see me
In the circus or zoo,
With my thick skin and trunk,
And ivory tusks, too.
I am an e__9__.

Twenty-six letters in strict order set,
You must learn me. I am the a__10__.

C **What do they do?** Write a word to complete each sentence.

A b__11__ carries traffic away from the city centre.
An o__12__ lives on the seabed before being gathered for food.
A p__13__ stands in Egypt as a great monument.
A s__14__ squirts or injects liquid into a vein.
A t__15__ prints letters by pressing keys on an instrument.

D **Group words.** Write a word to complete each group.

old-fashioned, aged, ancient, a__16__
wreckage, ruins, rubbish, d__17__
staff, truncheon, stick, b__18__
voucher, ticket, entry-form, c__19__
writing-desk, office, department, b__20__

E **What is in it?** Write a word to complete each sentence.

In a h__21__ residents are sleeping.
In a r__22__ diners are eating.
In a m__23__ courses for a meal are listed.
In an o__24__ are eggs and melted butter.
In a s__25__ are instruments for relaying pictures back to earth.